WILLIAM ZORACH IN HIS STUDIO

THE SCULPTURE OF WILLIAM ZORACH

By PAUL S. WINGERT

Department of Fine Arts and Archeology, Columbia University
NEW YORK CITY

PITMAN PUBLISHING CORPORATION

NEW YORK CHICAGO

1938

Acknowledgments

The writing of this book has been made possible through the generous supplying of the factual material by Mr. and Mrs. William Zorach. Credit is due for the excellent reproductions to the photographers Paul Hansen, Charles Sheeler, Carl Klein, Pinchos Horn, and Peter Juley, all of New York City. The author also wishes to express his gratitude to Mr. Edward L. Mills of Columbia University for reading the manuscript and for offering suggestions.

Table of Contents

THE SCULPTURE OF WILLIAM ZORACH

I Foreword

ADEQUATE galleries for the exhibition of sculpture are rare. Thus the public is not as well acquainted with the work of contemporary sculptors as it is with that of present-day painters. The publication of photographs, however, would partly relieve this situation; and it is for that purpose that the present corpus of photographs of the more important sculptures of William Zorach is herewith presented. It is hoped that the public in this way will become better acquainted with the work of one of the outstanding contemporary sculptors. In the text the desire has been to treat the factual material in as complete a fashion as possible, and to offer a systematic analytical interpretation of his principal works so as to show the intent of his sculpture and the position he occupies in the contemporary scene. It is earnestly hoped, therefore, that the general public will find something of interest in the following pages and that the student will find them helpful.

PAUL S. WINGERT

New York City
March, 1938

3

2 Introduction

WILLIAM ZORACH belongs to a pioneer group of contemporary sculptors who have interpreted sculpture to mean the art of carving stone, rather than that of modelling in a pliable material, such as clay. In the twenty years which have passed since his early experiments, this group of stone carvers has increased to include many of the younger generation, on whom Zorach has had considerable influence. The art of carving stone means, as is implied, the actual cutting of a form from the stone directly by the artist. Much of the finest sculpture of ancient times was produced in this way; but for the past few hundred years it has been the practise to model a figure first in a material easy to work and then to have a professional stone cutter copy the model mechanically in stone, the sculptor afterwards often polishing the finished work and sometimes making a few changes. It was in reaction against this practise that a group of sculptors returned to the method of direct carving in the stone. The advantage of this procedure is that, to cut directly in the stone, the artist must understand the intrinsic properties of his materials; and the more thorough this knowledge, the more adapted will the finished work be to the medium, and the more will it show the handiwork of the sculptor. This method of carving also necessitated to a certain extent

5

a revival and a restatement of the principles previously held regarding the function and character of the art.

IN the nineteenth century especially, sculpture had come to mean an imitative reproducing of nature, and this brought about an over-emphasis of the subject matter and a lack of consideration of the properties of the materials employed. For an art primarily restricted in subject matter to a reproduction of the human form, this emphasis upon the externals of the object reproduced tended to reduce to a minimum the larger plastic implications of form. Having recognized the evil days upon which the art had fallen, contemporary sculptors made an important contribution toward reestablishing sounder principles by reaffirming the character of sculpture as an expression of the subject matter in terms of the material; hence bringing the art into closer relationship with the material than it had been in the nineteenth century. Coupled with this contribution was the rediscovery, so to speak, of the proper function of sculpture as an enlargement of aesthetic experience. The emphasis given to the imitative and decorative character of a work, in which the accidental details of the subject were carefully pronounced and just as carefully arranged, was now discarded in favor of the more fundamental function a figure in stone could serve.

SINCE the art of sculpture has the human form as its principal subject matter, sculptors of recent years have realized that by interpreting the structural relationships between the component parts of a form held together in a design by a unifying linear and spatial rhythm and by expressing these relationships in plastic terms inherent in the material and in the structure of the form, they could again make sculpture interpret and express life. In this way a figure in stone would no longer be just an imitation of natural appearances. Rather, it would be an interpretation of the essential elements of a form as the artist perceives them, arranged in an interesting and expressive design. This was the point of view from which the direct carvers approached their art, and among these one of the most outstanding was William Zorach.

CHARACTERIZED by a strong human quality, his sculpture combines a deep sincerity and respect for life with a natural feeling for the arrangement of forms in a simple, strong, expressive design. The permanent character of human form in its fundamental relationships is what Zorach usually strives for in his figures. They retain to a remarkable degree the intrinsic qualities of the stone, the living spirit of his subjects, and the broad decorative elements common to both. He achieves this quality in his works partly through his acute sensitivity to the vibrancy of a line, to the expansive volume of a full curve, to the rhythmic relationships between forms and the space surrounding and separating them.

HIS sculpture has a solemn, calm, meditative spirit, comparable to that of the ancient Egyptians, the early Greeks, and the Chinese. Although he has learned much from a study of past styles, yet his art does not derive from any one of them but is an individual interpretation based on essential sculptural principles. His work is within the tradition of his art, and bridges the gap between the sincere sculptural expression of mediaeval times and today. His figures, nevertheless, are not of an age or a period, but express the permanent ageless qualities of form.

LIKE all sincere art, his sculpture retains the spirit and freshness of its original conception, and yet this spontaneity is restrained and calm. His forms are rich in development and filled with content. A sculpture of Zorach's should be seen again and again, at different times of the day, at different seasons, to understand the depth of interpretation in his work. Through his unselfish criticism and instruction, his influence on the younger generation has been considerable; and this influence will be increased when his sculptures are eventually placed in our public museums where they rightly belong.

3 Biographical Account

WILLIAM Zorach was born in the small Lithuanian town of Eurburg on February 28, 1887. When he was four years old his family emigrated to America and for three years lived in the Ohio village of Pat Clinton, near Cleveland, afterwards moving to that city. There, young Zorach attended the public schools; but life was so arduous for the family during these years that a good part of his time was spent on whatever work could be had to earn his own living. The circumstances of an orthodox and religious home environment knit the family by very close bonds of affection and kinship into a strong unit. Zorach was greatly influenced by this background of family devotion, and later, transferred to his own fireside, it contributed strongly to the sincere, unified emotion found in his sculpture, supplying him also with many of his themes.

THE future sculptor's art training began when a supervisor of art in the public schools of Cleveland perceived his unusual talent for drawing. He advised the boy to develop this talent, and in an effort to help young Zorach gave him a letter of introduction to the Morgan Lithograph Company of Cleveland. He was hired immediately at a weekly wage of three dollars—not, however, because of his ability

9

to draw, but rather because the company had just had a fire and needed a husky boy of Zorach's type to help clean up the débris. Nevertheless it provided him with an opportunity to observe the work going on around him, and he was fascinated by what he saw. This interest was rewarded shortly later when, at the age of fifteen, he was apprenticed by the same company, and at nothing a week for six months; afterwards, for the remainder of his three year period of apprenticeship, he was paid a nominal weekly wage. During these years, 1902-1905, Zorach studied at night at the Cleveland School of Art. Upon the completion of his term as apprentice, he was engaged as a lithographer by the same firm, a position which he retained until 1908. It was from these beginnings in commercial art that he developed the antipathy which he now has towards it as a vocation, but it was with the earnings of these three years as a commercial lithographer that he was permitted to further his training for the career which he now knew he wanted to pursue, namely, that of a creative artist. His chief interest then was drawing and painting, and in 1908 he went to New York, where he studied until 1910 in the National Academy of Design. While there, he won a medal for excellence in drawing and an honorable mention for his painting. The logical next step for a young artist in those days was Paris, which had long since supplanted Rome as the Mecca of American artists, and for that objective Zorach sailed in 1910.

PARIS in that year was a very vital place for a young, impressionable artist. The art world there was full of activity, the schools and studios excited with discussions of a new art and a new age. Free experiments in techniques and in the interpretation of form, with the avowed intention of abandoning the wornout precedents of the nineteenth century, characterized the work then being done there by the younger painters and sculptors. The Fauves ("Wild Animal") group with Matisse at their head was attracting much attention; the Salon des Indépendants exhibition was filled with work in the new modes; and the first Cubist exhibition was then being held. In these events Zorach soon began to participate, working in different schools and studios, and spending much time in the various museums, particularly the Louvre. The following spring found him settled in the south of France, where he remained for five months, painting. The results of these months show that he had learned much since his arrival in Europe, and that his sympathies were with the new movements. Four of his paintings of that spring were exhibited in the 1912 Salon d'Automne in Paris. By this time his funds were pretty well depleted and he returned to America in December of that year. While in Europe, however, Zorach became acquainted not only with the new art ideas, but also with the American art student, Marguerite Thompson, who later became Mrs. Zorach. An accomplished artist in her own right, she has been a constant source of inspiration and encouragement to him.

THE hardest task which confronts an artist faced him when he arrived in New York from Paris: the extremely difficult one of establishing himself as an artist—of becoming known to the collectors, the dealers, and the public, a particularly difficult business at that time in the American environment, essentially commercial in its art preferences and rather indifferent to original creative work. Thus, in spite of his distaste for it, Zorach had to turn again to commercial lithography as a means of livelihood, returning to Cleveland and to the same firm with which he had begun his apprenticeship ten years before, the Morgan Lithograph Company. During that year, however, he had in Cleveland the first showing of his work in America. As in his earlier days, he knew that the greatest opportunity for a young artist in this country at that time was in New York City, so to that city he returned the following year—and again with his earnings as a commercial artist.

IN 1913, he exhibited his paintings in two important shows in New York—the now famous Armory Show and the MacDowell Club Show. It was through these exhibitions that his name first came to the attention of the collectors, the art critics, and the general public.

DURING the next seven years Zorach painted constantly, spending his winters in New York and his summers in out-of-the-way country places in New England. Gradually he became well known as a painter and his work frequently appeared in gallery shows, principally in the early exhibitions of the Society of Independent Artists, the Whitney Studio Club, and the 1914, 1915, and 1916 shows at the Daniel Gallery. His future career in this art seemed particularly assured. But he had never felt that painting was his natural medium. He had always been an experimenter, assimilating the new ideas, methods and approaches; and although his work showed a constant progression, yet he had not arrived at a definite style—that is, not what one could call a "Zorach style." Nevertheless, his painting was brilliant in conception and execution, and he would have arrived at a fully developed manner had not a new interest directed his activities into other channels.

In the summer of 1917, while camping on the abandoned Echo Farm in New Hampshire, Zorach became interested in the possibilities of the form in a design he was cutting as a wood-block, and he developed it into a relief carving (Plate 1). This panel, of Butternut wood, was his first piece of sculpture. The following summer he produced a work in the round, a small terra cotta "Walking Baby" (Plate 2), together with two relief medallions and a modelled and carved bowl. At first in the nature of a hobby, this interest in the new medium of sculpture soon became more and more absorbing; and although his greater efforts remained devoted to painting, nevertheless between 1919 and 1922 he carved ten free-standing figures in wood, varying in size from a very small one of about six inches to a three foot "Mother and Child" group in mahogany (Plate 9).

It was during these four years that Zorach realized that sculpture was a natural medium for him, and as a result of this discovery he abandoned oil painting in 1922 and embarked upon the career of a sculptor. That he should have decided in favor of this art is not surprising, for an examination of his painting of this time reveals an increasing interest in the plastic possibilities of form, which becomes most marked after 1918. Hence it seems just to consider this exchange of media not so much as an absolute change but rather as a logical evolution from painting to sculpture.

NEVERTHELESS, to take such a step required courage and firm conviction. He had never had any formal training in sculpture, and had to discover for himself the handling of tools, the nature of different materials, and the methods of approach to the problems of the art. But to this new medium he devoted himself with renewed energy and his progress was extremely rapid. There soon emerged in his work a style distinctly his own. Based on a knowledge of materials, a sense of design, and a firm realization of the plastic qualities of the human form, his sculpture showed an implicit sincerity and a depth of penetration which gave to his figures a permanent vitality and filled them with a timeless meaningfulness.

ZORACH's sculpture was first shown at the Kraushaar Gallery in 1924, and again there in 1926 and 1928; and for some years thereafter he exhibited annually at the Downtown Gallery, where in 1931 his show of direct sculpture was one of the most interesting shows of the year. Other important showings of his work have been held at the Whitney Museum of American Art in New York City, at the Chicago Art Institute, and at the Cleveland Museum, the Newark Museum, and other museums in the East and West. By 1930 he had become widely known as an extremely able sculptor; and since then his reputation has been increasing with the progression of his art, until today he is one of the outstanding contemporary sculptors. Many of his works are owned by museums and private collectors in this country, and he is a member of the American Society of Painters, Sculptors and Gravers.

DURING these years of activity as a sculptor, however, he has not entirely given up painting. On the contrary, he has achieved a notable reputation as a water colorist, his show in this medium at the Downtown Gallery in 1932 bringing most forcibly to public attention this side of his work. In the same year, moreover, he received the Logan Medal and the $500 purchase prize for water colors at the 12th International Water Color Exhibition at the Art Institute of Chicago. Many examples of this phase of Zorach's career are also in museums and private collections; while in the fall of 1937 four of his landscapes, a type of subject particularly suited to his water color style, were selected to form a part of the contemporary American art exhibit which is to open in Paris in the summer of 1938. The greater part of his painting is now done during his summer residence in Maine; and his water colors contain, generally, the same solid construction and integrated design as his sculptures, and show him to be a colorist of importance.

PERHAPS the best known of his sculptures is the large marble "Mother and Child" (Plates 23, 24), which he executed between 1927 and 1930. It was with this work, shown first at the Downtown Gallery and later at various other places in New York City, that he won the Logan Medal and $1500 prize for sculpture at the Chicago Art Institute in 1931. Curiously enough, however, this magnificent work, embodying as it does the most characteristic elements of his style, remains in the possession of the artist, a testimony of the difficult position occupied by sculptors in our present-day culture. Among his more recent works should be mentioned the large marble "Benjamin Franklin" (Plate 47), unveiled during the fall of 1937 in the Benjamin Franklin Post Office Building in Washington, D. C., and the commissions upon which he is engaged for the New York World's Fair in 1939. At the present time he is bringing to completion a monumental male and female group, carved directly in beautiful Italian marble; this work will probably be exhibited in the fall of 1938.

ZORACH now lives on West 9th Street in New York City and has his studio on West 15th Street. He is a prodigious worker, and is happy only when he is busily engaged. During recent years, he has somehow found time to devote considerable efforts to teaching, through which he has been of much influence on the younger generation of sculptors, principally, since 1929, through his sculpture classes at the Art Students League of New York City. And for many years he has also acted as art supervisor in a group of progressive schools in and around New York City.

4 Chronological Development and Analysis of Zorach's Sculpture

THERE is much that could be learned from a day-to-day description of the work of an artist. From such an account, one could follow the emergence of an idea as the solution of a problem and the gradual growth of that idea into the finished work; one could see the development of the technical facility of the artist; and, above all, one could understand the slow evolution of style—that is to say, the way in which an artist translates his ideas into expressive compositions. This method, however, is wholly impracticable. Instead, an examination of the more important works, taken in their chronological order, is highly instructive; and this is the method which will be followed in a study of the sculptures of Zorach.

IT is seldom that more than a suggestion of the mature manner of an artist appears in his earliest works. Generally, they are too closely related to the manner of his masters to have much to say in their own right. The first efforts of Zorach, however, have no reminiscences of the work of a "master," since he had no formal training in sculpture, but show to a surprising degree a sense of design and scale, of simplified, compact form and volume which follow through all of his subsequent work. In spite of linear tendency in his

"Decorative Wooden Relief Panel" of 1917 (Plate 1) an interesting plastic design and a suggestion of solid form has begun to emerge. These qualities had been apparent in his painting for some years, and it is not to be wondered at that they are apparent in his first work of sculpture.

MORE remarkable and far more significant, however, was the appearance the following summer of the small "Walking Baby" (Plate 2). The first piece of sculpture in the round attempted by him, this little figure, measuring scarcely eight inches, has the scale and the simplified, solid rendering of a monumental work, together with the sincerity and the sturdy spontaneity of so much of his later sculpture. For the first free-standing figure by a self-trained artist, surprisingly few technical imperfections are apparent. The "Walking Baby" was originally modelled in clay, and it was not until the following year, 1919, that he carved his first work in the round, the two-foot wood carving entitled "Man with Two Wives" (Plate 3).

BETWEEN the four years 1919 to 1922, Zorach made eight wood carvings; and it was during these years that he definitely realized that sculpture was his proper medium. In comparison with his earlier attempts, the "Man with Two Wives" is a pretentious work. The original shape of the cedar post suggested the design, and in this respect it is a good example of the application of a principle followed by Zorach and other modern sculptors: that the original shape of the material should exercise an influence on the design of a work. Moreover, in this early group appears the sculptor's inherent feeling for and understanding of the qualities of the material and of the form natural to it. The feeling of plastic sincerity already so evident in his first two efforts is here fully expressed, although again one finds technical imperfections and a certain suggestion of striving for expression in a medium with which the artist is still not too familiar.

THE next year, 1920, while camping in Yosemite National Park, Zorach carved, chiefly with a penknife, the small free-standing wooden figure of the "Artist's Daughter" (Plate 4). Cut in sprucewood, it is of about the same size as the "Walking Baby" modelled two years before, but when compared with this earlier figure it shows the development towards a true sculptural conception which had taken place in that short time in the artist's handling of a three-dimensional medium. In place of a generalized modelling, this wood carving is developed from an analysis of the structural elements of the little form, these features in turn being expressed in simplified terms so as to accentuate their chief characteristics. The completed figure is a totality of the various parts to which each contributes its essential character, the result being a figure structural, as a work of architecture, with each part as significant and as well expressed. Already in this work the scale, the individual rendering of the parts and their articulation into a plastic whole suggest the peculiar characteristics of Negro sculpture. This stylistic analogy becomes even more apparent in the three wood carvings which he did at Provincetown the following summer, in 1921.

THE first, the figure of a "Young Boy" (Plate 5), is a fine expression of these qualities. In this work the analysis of the essential character of the component parts of the figure leads to an expression employing amplification, exaggeration, and distortion for purposes of a more unified, plastic, architectural rendering to a degree that suggests an especially close relationship to primitive Negro wood carvings. Each part and feature is distinct and clearly expressed with economy of detail, the design of the figure as a whole compact and well suited to the material, and the scale impressive and significant. Very similar in treatment are the other two figures dating from this summer, the "Young Girl" (Plate 6) and the "Figure of a Child" (Plate 7).

THESE three works are extremely important for an understanding of Zorach's later sculptures, since in them he displays for the first time truly plastic conceptions. He is overcoming his unfamiliarity with a new medium, and is actually designing three-dimensional figures. More important, however, is the vigor and strength of his carving, and the vitality and expressiveness which result. It should be explained, regarding the suggestion of similarities between these works and primitive Negro sculptures, that this was not merely fortuitous. At this time Zorach was much interested in the wood carvings from Africa and there is no doubt that they contributed much to this phase of his plastic development. But having learned so much from these primitive carvings, his three remaining works of this formative period, 1919 to 1922, show a steady progress in the application of these principles.

CHRONOLOGICAL DEVELOPMENT AND ANALYSIS

THESE three figures were carved in mahogany in 1922. In them all uncertainty and sense of striving in technical matters disappear, and there exists for the first time that sincere and important emotional quality which is so closely associated with most of his subsequent work. "Floating Figure" (Plate 8) represents a nude female figure, relaxed and buoyant, floating on her back. It resulted from many observations made by the sculptor of swimming forms. Composed in extremely simplified, generalized terms, the emphasis is upon an expressive volume, in which form flows into form. The character of the design is perfectly compatible with the nature of the wood, the grain of which is beautifully handled; while the compactness of the figure and the free use of distortion show to what degree he has profited by his studies of primitive wood carvings. Also, the subtle quality of the undulating silhouette is an important element in the final achievement of this work, and it remains essentially a decorative figure, with, nevertheless, a clear statement of masses and volumes.

THE second of these mahogany figures is his first sculptural rendering of the "Mother and Child" theme (Plate 9) and represents a developed composition with more than a single figure. An arrangement of solid, sturdy forms replaces in this work the suave treatment of the "Floating Figure." Distortion, amplification, and deformation are resorted to, in order to express within the confines of the original block the truly three-dimensional design. It is his first handling of a complex design in which the spatial relationships of form to form, of area to area are carefully worked out,

21

with the two-fold objective of creating forms natural to the material, and expressive of the human emotion so inherent in such a group. The surfaces remain generalized, with perhaps a suggestion here and there of development.

THE last work of this period is the mahogany "Boy and Girl Group" (Plate 10), a compactly designed piece of wood carving expressing vividly the personality and the permanent reality of these two small figures. As in all three mahogany carvings dating from this year, the scale here is of monumental proportions, although actually each of these works is about three feet high. In the treatment of form this "Boy and Girl Group" differs considerably from that of "Mother and Child," each part being rounded, and amplified to express its essential quality of mass and volume. Furthermore, although the sturdy forms are still simplified and generalized, considerably more surface treatment is resorted to. Also, there is apparent in the handling of the heads a tendency towards a greater naturalism and a more conspicuous decorative treatment than in most of his later works of such sculptural qualities. Again, the group is designed by carefully arranging the volume of the forms in terms of a new plastic expressiveness and rhythm, keeping the group well within the original limits of the block. This carving is, moreover, an extremely spontaneous one, and preserves in sincere, unmistakable fashion the tender, human quality of the sculptor's subjects.

THE works which have so far been considered were all of them accomplished during the summers, Zorach still devoting his winters in the city to painting, and show a developing technique in this new medium, and a genuine feeling for three-dimensional design. He had now decided conclusively that sculpture was his natural medium for artistic expression, and in the summer of 1923 at Provincetown he carved his first pieces in stone. The initial venture in stone carving was in white Italian marble, the head of the "Artist's Daughter" (Plate 11). It is essentially a decorative and naturalistic rendering of the subject, to a greater degree, in fact, than is usual in Zorach's work. The hair is arranged in a simplified pattern enframing the delicately modelled face, the conception being a tender characterization, with the features handled so as to conclude a decorative whole. Especially noticeable in this respect is the repetition in the treatment of the eyes of the full curves of the mouth. Here the sculptor followed a procedure which he has followed very often since: he cut the work directly in the stone without first working up a preliminary sketch model in clay. It represents, then, the original conception as the artist himself worked it out in the material, and not a translation of ideas formulated in a more pliable material. It should be observed that again in this head Zorach has kept his form solid, with a firm, continuous profile, and with no voids within this line; thus creating a truly sculptural design that is particularly suitable to his material. This portrait marks the beginning of a year, the first one, devoted entirely to sculpture. However, with the exception of another portrait, "Head of a Woman" (Plate 12), cut in pink Tennessee marble, it was the only stone carving he did that year.

HE continued, on the other hand, with the material in which he had started to work out his conceptions of form, that is, in wood. The "Figure of a Girl" (Plate 13) was carved in lignum vitae, a very hard wood with a black core and a beautiful grain. Zorach designed his form to bring out these qualities of the wood, producing a figure of simplified and arbitrary parts, but one of grace and beauty of design, in which the natural qualities of the wood (the color and grain) give added interest to the disposition of forms and the fine linear rhythm.

SHORTLY after this figure, the sculptor did one of his best known works, the "Pegasus" (Plate 14), now in the Whitney Museum in New York City. Carved in walnut, this small work represents a new idea in his art, and an extremely important one for the development of his later work. This idea was to amplify, or to increase, the volume of his forms in order to gain increased sculptural qualities. To accomplish this, it was necessary to simplify the forms to a greater degree than he had done up to this time and to express his subjects in a more generalized fashion. This meant, to a certain degree, the abandoning of a decorative quality based on a naturalism which is apparent in many of his earlier works. It also meant a further analysis of form in order to determine its essential character. This, then, was the intent of this little group, as it has since been of the greater part of Zorach's sculpture. "Pegasus" is perhaps his most pretentiously designed wood carving. The simple, solid forms are built up in a system of balance and spatial relations, with the position, description, and deformation of parts which are essential to the effectiveness of the whole. Again it should be observed that the work is kept solid, with no openings appearing within the profile. Similar in manner is the "Kiddie Car" (Plate 15) in rosewood, carved at the same time. Here the forms seem even more simplified and enlarged. The result is an emphatically sculptural work, with a more basic, less generalized interpretation of the subject.

ZORACH's first truly monumental stone sculpture was the "Portrait of Mrs. Zorach" (Plate 18). Directly carved in pink Tennessee marble, it was started in the second year of his career as a sculptor, in 1924, and finished in 1926. It is only slightly over life-size; but by means of a general description of features, broad treatment of planes, and retention of the qualities of the material, the sculptor has produced a work of inherent mass and expressed volume. The characterization of the subject is strong, sincere, with a spirit of eternalized spontaneity in its conception. Effective as a contrast to the completely carved face, the hair is rough-cut, as is also the base, so that the stony character of the marble is preserved and the structural character of the head is accented. Technically the head is magnificent, and as a portrait it is a superb characterization, infusing the stone to a remarkable degree with the quality of life.

DATING from the same year (1926) in which this portrait was finished, and handled in a very similar manner, is the pink Tennessee marble bust entitled "Child with Cat" (Plate 19). This is another good example of Zorach's direct carving in stone. It began without any preliminary sketches whatever. The design changed and developed as the sculptor worked with the block of stone until there emerged this compact, interesting design of a girl supporting a cat against her right shoulder. Designed in large, ample plastic areas, and with a breadth of surface modelling, this work has genuine sculptural and monumental character. The sense of the essential permanent character of his forms is again apparent; while the spirit of spontaneity and the quality of life are clearly evident. This is especially true in the rendering of the cat.

FOR some years the possibility of the cat as a sculptural form had interested Zorach. There had always been fine specimens in his home, where he had observed and had made many drawings of them. Hence he came to know the basic character and form of the cat, not as individuals, but rather the formal elements common to all cats. This is what he has given here, in intense, plastic, simplified fashion. The design is well integrated, and again the mass within the enclosing silhouette is solid, unbroken by voids.

WHILE in Maine the following year, he carved in maplewood the full length portrait of his young daughter, the work known as "Figure of Young Girl in Short Dress" (Plate 21). Based on many studies, this figure again shows the interest of the sculptor in universal form, in place of a particular description of an individual figure. Rounded, ample forms again dominate, being those which Zorach recognizes as best suited to sculptural expression. The design is compact and balanced, and the decorative element, never neglected by the sculptor, is apparent not as surface decoration but as a sculptural quality, forming an integral part of his arrangement. The silhouette of the figure is especially simple, and the volume of the form well expressed.

DURING the fall of that same year, 1927, Zorach began working on a clay sketch for a "Mother and Child" group (Plate 22). The generic idea of the human relationship between mother and child had interested him for some years as a subject for his own sculpture; and this group represents the second stage (the wood carving of 1922 being the first) in the development of a sculptural expression of this motive. The direction in which his style had been progressing—towards more solid, ample, sculptural forms—was carried a bit farther in this work. Here he achieves a three-dimensional character by designing the forms to move, as it were, about a central axis and in this fashion they are so disposed and built up as to carry the eye around the figures, thus compelling the spectator to move around the group in order to understand the full meaning of the forms.

ALTHOUGH differing in certain elements of design, this small sketch served as a preliminary study for the large monumental "Mother and Child" (Plates 23 and 24), hence the ideas in the process of being worked out in this smaller one appear in a more developed state in the larger work. Carved directly and entirely by Zorach himself in rich warm pink Spanish marble, this large rendering of the idea followed immediately after the smaller sketch and occupied the sculptor from 1927 to 1930. It is a genuinely monumental piece of stone carving, and represents one of the most important pieces of direct carving by a modern sculptor. Contrary to the usual procedure in monumental works, the sculptor made no full-sized plaster model. Instead, the idea grew and slowly emerged as he progressed with the work. As in the smaller predecessor of this theme, the solid, rounded forms seem to revolve slowly around a central axis; while here a rich monumentality is achieved by the carefully worked out relationships between solids and voids, and by the interplay of a flowing linear rhythm. To attain this sculptural expressiveness required, as the work progressed, a constantly careful study for the development of volume and mass in the forms. When this was accomplished, the forms were then defined by planes, broadly and delicately modelled—a method dictated by the beautiful quality of the marble. The hair of both figures is again left in the rough, to form a contrast to the finished surfaces below and to describe the general character of hair; and the features of the faces are generalized in treatment but are filled with a quiet and deep human sentiment. The work as a whole represents a fine rendering of a subject appropriate to the material, in which the forms seem to develop naturally out of the stone, taking on the character of the marble and giving to it the warm feeling of life and of human tenderness. It is a truly monumental group, and to be seen adequately should be placed in a large well-lighted room, so that the spectator could walk around it and study it in detail.

WHILE Zorach was engaged upon this work, he carved the three-quarter figure of the "Artist's Daughter" (Plate 26), now in the Whitney Museum in New York City. A life-sized figure cut directly in Georgia pink marble, the subject is interpreted in terms of extreme simplification. The forms, in fact, have an elemental character, so general is their description; no wealth of defining planes exists here, but only the most broad and primary ones. Even the features of the face are not clear in their definition, appearing to be just emerging from the matrix of the stone. This, in fact, is the general character of the work: the sculptor emphasizes the nature of the material by not carrying the description of the form beyond a certain point. The effect is as sculptural and as elemental as an early Egyptian carving, and preserves a like quality of "stoniness." Nevertheless the work is infused with tender, human feeling and sincerity of expression.

DURING the eight years which have followed the first showing of the "Mother and Child" at the Downtown Gallery in New York City, Zorach has been extremely productive. Although he has done from time to time an occasional wood carving, most of his work of this period has been in stone, direct carvings in a variety of materials ranging from easily cut marbles to hard native sandstones and granites. He has always made a close study of materials, and seldom does he create a design which is not appropriate to the material.

A FINE example of this is to be found in the portrait head entitled "Hilda" (Plate 27). Directly carved in a rich yellow-brown Italian marble known as Jaune Nile, the rounded forms which predominate actually enhance the beautiful quality of the stone, and seem to grow naturally from it. For this he made no preliminary clay sketches but worked from a drawing of the subject. The bony structure of the head is most distinctly and simply defined, and the facial features are interpreted for their intrinsic sculptural qualities. Expressed in terms of the universal, plastic elements common to all heads, the individualization of the subject is minimized, appearing in the disposition of the features within the bounds of the general design, and in the expressiveness of the mouth.

A COMPARISON of this work with the earlier portrait of Mrs. Zorach (Plate 18) will show the extent to which this generic interpretation has developed. The surface planes of the portrait of "Hilda" are very broad and general in treatment, the work being essentially clear and direct, strongly plastic and expressive of the character of the stone. It is first and foremost a piece of sculpture. Moreover, the head has a marked plastic decorative quality comparable to that of many of the primitive African masks; while the spirit of life so inherent in it makes it a strongly human work. This portrait was done in 1931.

THE same year, during the summer in Maine, the sculptor carved from a natural green granite boulder, picked up along a road, one of his many expressive cats. This "Cat" (Plate 28), curled as though asleep in front of the fire, grew naturally from the shape of the boulder. Cut from a material extremely hard to work, the forms are very generalized, with a minimum of description, embodying only the elements most necessary to bring out the form of a cat in this pose. The result shows that fusion of subject with material which Zorach constantly strives for in his sculpture. He desired here to preserve to the utmost the natural shape of the stone and to express that shape in terms of an interesting plastic form which had meaning in itself and so could add meaning and interest to the material. He has achieved a work entirely successful in this respect; small though it is, the simple, general forms give the work scale and a sculptural sense of mass and volume, commensurate with the character of the material. Zorach has of recent years frequently used for his smaller sculptures Maine boulders of this sort because of the interest he has in materials, and in the properties native to this particular material, and because of the interesting color and texture of these "native" stones.

IN 1932 Zorach received a commission which gave him an opportunity to do a monumental work. This resulted in his now famous figure in the Radio City Music Hall in New York City, the "Spirit of the Dance" (Plate 29). In a new material, cast aluminum, this was first modelled in clay and shows that the sculptor has a mastery of this technique as well as of direct carving in stone. It is expressed in more naturalistic terms than usual in a Zorach figure and represents in rounded, clearly defined shapes the stately, grave movement of the dance. The forms again revolve slowly around a central axis, as in the "Mother and Child" (see Plate 23), so that the spectator must move slowly around the figure to perceive its full meaning. The design utilizes the voids between the forms just as clearly as the solid masses of the forms themselves, thus creating a rich pattern of movement in space, and a figure of which each part is a clearly described form in itself, structural and necessary for the final unity of the figure and the expressiveness of the subject. It is as logically and lucidly composed as a work of architecture, and yet in spite of its stately quality it has a strong spirit of spontaneity, and carries a full conviction of life in its forms. The modelling and the surfaces are simple and fluid, and appropriate to the character of the new material; while the decorative element, although strong, is expressed in restrained and sculptural terms. A feature in the lounge of the Music Hall, the figure shows the magnificent technical ability of Zorach, the dignity of his art in expressing fundamental, human elements, and his fine sense of structure and design.

THIS quality of structure appears in another work of the same year, the "Torso" in Labrador granite (Plate 30), now in the Whitney Museum in New York City. Here the forms are reduced to their most elemental shapes, suitable to a material of the hardness of granite, and the whole is rendered as a strong plastic unit. The areas and forms are clearly defined in the broadest and most general terms, and the work has an intrinsic, permanent character in keeping with the nature of the material.

THE human element so evident in the work of Zorach appears in two works which he did in 1933. The first of these, a child astride and caressing a large dog, is entitled "Affection" (Plate 32). Carved directly in York Fossil, a dark blue-black marble, this small group grew from a quick sketch which the sculptor made of a similar subject. With all of the spontaneity appropriate to such a theme, this work escapes falling into the category of a pretty recording of a whimsical scene through the handling of the sturdy rounded forms. To them he gives a sculptural quality expressing their monumental volume and the heavy mass of the material. Nothing of the accidental and the pretty appears in this description; by his simplified handling of the forms and their arrangement in a structural group the artist has created a work well adapted to a material beautiful in itself through its texture and color.

THE second of these expressive works of that year is the monumental clay group entitled "The Embrace" (Plate 33). It represents the fundamental element in the love between man and woman, an expression of an elemental human relationship, fraught with emotional significance, as is the relationship between mother and child. There appears here the full meaning of Zorach's desire to select for his sculpture subjects as permanent and ageless as the stones in which they are carved. Not concerned with a description of realistic elements, he has avoided the sensual and the insignificant by creating figures filled with the vibrant dignity of life in one of its most sacred and meaningful moments. The design is masterful, and makes clear the steady development which the sculptor has made in his ability to arrange form in an expressive and at the same time a sculptural, structural fashion.

CHARACTERISTICALLY the figures are designed around a central axis, and the solid areas of the full, rounded forms are disposed in carefully balanced, rhythmical manner, while the spaces between them create an interesting pattern of solids and voids. The interplay of forms, so expressive of their volume and mass, the spatial relationships between them, and the play of linear rhythms make of this a group extremely interesting from the point of view of design alone. One is again forced to move around the figures in order to appreciate fully the complete meaning; thus it is in the truest sense a piece of sculpture in three dimensions. Expressed in terms of their individual parts, the forms are described in their elementary shapes, clearly delineated by very general, broad planes, the group as a whole making an extremely compact unit. Zorach has worked this out as a clay model of monumental proportions, using both a modelling and a carving technique in treating the material. It is the sculptor's desire to produce this work in stone, to which material the design is so appropriate.

ZORACH has done relatively little portrait sculpture, but one head carved in 1933 in granite (Plate 34) will show to what degree his feeling for the character of materials determines the final form of such works. Compared with the portrait of "Hilda" (Plate 27), this head has a harder delineation of feature, no delicate surface treatment, and a more generalized rendering of the subject—a method of treatment more suitable to the hard character of granite than to the softer quality of marble. Otherwise, the approach to the problem of portraiture is approximately the same: the desire to create first a work of sculpture, and secondly to capture the important features and character of the subject.

IN 1934 Zorach carved directly in York Fossil the small but monumental group, "Child on a Pony" (Plate 40). Again the sculptor worked from pencil drawings and not from a preliminary model; and again he has created a sculpture filled with the quiet dignity of life, and expressive of the character of his material. This work should be compared with "Affection," carved in the same material in 1933. In the earlier group, a very spontaneous and human interpretation, the description of the forms is more complete than in the later work, where the content is of greater dignity and the subject matter capable of more elemental expression. Carved with no open spaces between the forms, and contained within a continuous, simple enclosing line, the "Child on a Pony" is so designed as to be seen from one position without moving around the figure. The purpose of this sculpture is to express the expansive volume and the solid mass of the contrasting forms of the girl and the pony in a material capable of sustaining them. Ample surface planes of delicate modelling define the forms in very simple terms; and again the work is knit into a compact unit. Using a material of interesting texture and color and susceptible to a high polish, the sculptor has accentuated these qualities by leaving the spaces between the forms, which would normally have been cut away, in the rough, thus creating an interesting contrast of surfaces and colors. As usual in his interpretation of a subject, this group is not so much the expression of a specific pony and a certain child, but rather of a generic conception of the character common to all ponies and to all children, expressed in these large, amplified forms so as to give the essential structure a greater sculptural dignity.

DURING the summer of 1935, Zorach carved from a natural Maine boulder a "Granite Cat" (Plate 42). This should be compared with the "Granite Hound" (Plate 39) cut the summer before, and also with the "Cat" carved in 1931, both of these works made from natural Maine boulders. The more recent "Cat," and the "Hound," are different in treatment from the earlier Cat, the later works being carried to a much higher finish, and defined with a great deal more surface description. In them the sculptor has again followed the natural shapes of the boulders but not so completely as in the earlier works; while the high finish, although it does bring out one of the fundamental characteristics of the material, seems to make them more decorative and slightly less fundamental expressions of either the subject matter or of the material. Moreover, the clearer description of form in the "Granite Cat" creates a design of smaller plastic areas, which is perhaps more interesting, although a bit more obvious than the earlier work. On the other hand, this Cat is so intent on life that it must be considered a fine example of his more developed style.

THE following year, Zorach carved another "Cat." This one, cut directly in Swedish granite, is the one in the Metropolitan Museum in New York City (Plate 44). An extremely expressive and impressive work, this represents one of his most complete realizations in a hard durable material of the essential form of the cat. A monumental, dignified rendering worthy of being compared with the Mesopotamian animal sculpture in the same museum, this work resulted from a similar method of analysis of the object for its fundamental character, adapting it to the material in which the work is cut. The design is in simple, generalized terms, expressed with a minimum of modelling and a maximum of volume, the figure as a whole enclosed in an interesting, clearly defined silhouette. The description of forms here and the finish given to the material is mid-way between the two earlier natural granite boulder cats, just considered above. A worthy example of the sculptor's art this figure, because of its subject matter, obviously does not have the content of a work such as the "Mother and Child," or the "Embrace." The technique shows that he has attained a remarkable mastery of an extremely difficult material; while the design attests to his ability to arrange a subject so as to bring out the qualities of the material.

DURING his career as a sculptor, Zorach has not had the opportunity to do much monumental or architectural sculpture; and yet in his studio exists a plaster sketch model of an "Abraham Lincoln" (Plate 45) which contains the quality of just that sort of sculpture. Cut, rather than modelled in clay, this figure is the result of many close studies of the character and personality of Lincoln. Of powerful architectural forms, of rich variety from the square shapes of the legs to the rounded forms of the arms and torso, it is a work of tremendous monumental scale and capable of forming part of an architectural setting, or of being the central figure of an expansive vista. The forms as they now appear are only in the sketch stage, it is true, but from them we can derive a clear idea of the volume and the mass which such a figure would have when worked out, preferably directly cut, in a permanent material. The character of the man Lincoln as we know him is well expressed in powerful, human terms, without any superficial detail or accidental descriptive elements. The figure seems to emerge from the matrix of the material with which it is partly fused, and just enough emphasis is given to significant parts, such as the strong, able hands, to make it an extremely expressive interpretation. The design has Zorach's usual simplicity and clarity, and is worked out in architectural, structural terms.

THIS work was done in 1936; and the following year Zorach completed the sketch model of his now famous "Pioneer Family Group" (Plate 46) as his entry in the Dallas, Texas, competition of that year. A strongly integrated group of four figures, this is one of the best examples of his recent style. Filled with a deep feeling for the human relationships of a closely knit family group, bound closer together because of the hardships of a hostile environment, the forms are rendered in terms of their essential characters. The design of the work is extremely clear and well developed, so that each of the parts is closely related to the well unified whole. Forms balance forms, and the spatial relationships between them are carefully worked out, so that the group creates an interesting pattern of lines, of formal solid areas, of integrated form. The figures are interpreted in their most elementary shapes, amplification and distortion being resorted to in order to express better the character of the forms, the human relationships between them, and the intensely emotional note. Of monumental scale, this group, if the sculptor had had the opportunity to carve it in a more permanent material, would no doubt have been an extremely impressive sculptural work. But the Dallas Committee had to recall their first decision in favor of it, and the group was finally rejected.

IN 1937, Zorach brought to completion his figure of "Benjamin Franklin" (Plate 47) which had been commissioned in 1935 by the Treasury Department Art Projects Committee for the Postmaster General's Reception Hall in the new Benjamin Franklin Post Office in Washington, D. C. Carved in Tennessee marble, this seven and one half foot figure developed from much intensive research by the sculptor in an effort to arrive at an understanding of the physical characteristics of the man and of his personality and temperament.

ZORACH made many small clay sketches before arriving at a satisfactory design for this figure, and then contrary to his usual custom made a full scale model worked out in detail. From this model he made the figure, employing in this instance for the only time in his career the practice of pointing—mechanically transferring from the clay model to the block of marble the important measurements and features by means of guiding points. It also represents the only realistic and conventionally descriptive work which he has done; but the detail is handled fairly broadly, and in spite of the realistic manner some feeling for the material is evident. Moreover, the design is not typical of Zorach but is an adaptation of the conventional approach to this type of statue. A certain decorative treatment necessary for a figure of this sort further diminishes the true Zorach character. The statue, however, was a public commission and to the terms of the contract the sculptor was bound to conform.

SINCE the completion and installation of the "Benjamin Franklin," Zorach has finished and exhibited a preliminary sketch model for a "Fountain of Horses" (Plate 48). Fifteen figures participate in this small sketch, the size of which makes it difficult to comment on how the forms would develop in the completed work. It is sufficiently clear, however, that action is the keynote of the composition. This develops from the right and left in a sort of triangular pedimental fashion to an apex which is slightly off center, the main figure of the work being the female rider directly in the center of the composition, who stands in front of the other groups. All of the figures, men and animals alike, are handled in a strongly architectural fashion, with an interplay of rounded and block-like forms. The composition in spite of the number of figures (it seems crowded, perhaps because of the scale of this small sketch) has a certain unity, and the forms are created with a great deal of inherent power and an implied meaningfulness. This, however, remains at the moment just a sketch model, and no plans for its completion in permanent form have been made.

DURING the summer of 1938, Zorach expects to bring to completion an important monumental group which he began in the summer of 1934. This is a direct carving in beautiful Jaune Nile marble of a male and female group (Plate 49), which could justifiably be called "Prelude to Life." As in the "Mother and Child" and the "Embrace," this group expresses the sacred relationship between two figures. Arranged in an interlocking design, the forms create an interesting spatial and linear pattern, and are filled with a sense of brooding. The forms are simplified in description, solid and structural; and the group has the qualities of Zorach's mature manner.

FROM this chronological account of his more important work, the development of certain characteristics of his art have been observed, such as, among other things, the arrangement of figures in a lucid, interesting design; the desire to interpret form as formal relationships, infused with the spirit of life; and the interest in materials in general and the preference for certain ones in particular. Having thus followed the physical development of his sculpture, it is now desirable to discuss its spirit—its meaning and content, and to formulate and define his style.

5 Interpretation and Style

SCULPTURE can be grouped into two classes, first, the creative, original work—in which the artist approaches his problem from a personal point of view, desiring to interpret his forms as expressive of his own experience and understanding of life; and, secondly, the academic, popular work —in which the sculptor follows the patterns established for the interpretation of a subject, his forms consequently being comparatively impersonal. In either case, it is not a matter for contempt if a sculptor follows one rather than the other approach, since that is generally inherent in his temperament. It does matter, on the other hand, if an uncertainty of craftsmanship is apparent, for that imposes a limitation upon the artist. Nevertheless, critics of sculpture usually extol one type at the expense of the other, often without explaining what the intrinsic qualities of a work are, or without evaluating these qualities in terms of the character of the subject matter. Although the enjoyment of all art should be just as personal a matter as one's conception of religion, an analysis of a work of art is capable of adding to that fund of enjoyment; since it may open new vistas, it may increase one's awareness of subtleties of expression. The sculpture of William Zorach falls into the creative, original category, and can best be understood through a close examination of his monumental marble "Mother and Child" (Plates 23 and 24), in which the most characteristic elements of his mature style appear.

FOR a sculptor who generally carves directly in stone as Zorach does, the selection of a material appropriate to the subject, or conversely, of a subject appropriate to the material, is of prime importance. That necessitates an understanding of materials and of the forms most suitable for bringing out their inherent nature. It also imposes on the sculptor the necessity of analyzing form in terms of its expressive plastic qualities and of selecting a material capable of allowing them their greatest development. In other words, a material and subject matter must be selected which have certain things in common; the more they have in common the more apt the work is to become a meaningful piece of sculpture. Hence it is necessary to consider briefly the intrinsic qualities of the principal materials used by Zorach and why he has produced certain forms in a given material rather than in another.

MARBLE has been used for sculpture more than any other stone. A solid substance, generally with a fine grain, it is a comparatively soft stone and one easily worked. It is capable, because of its solid composition, of expressing expansive, rounded forms delicately modelled, and of taking a high surface polish. Thus a subject most suitable for marble would be one which, in its greatest expression, demanded a statement of rounded form, of subtle transitions of surface modelling, allowing for a play of light over the surface, and of a decorative, polished finish to the stone. Because of the comparative softness of this material, a greater amount of detail can be rendered, and a greater decorative quality attained, producing the ever present danger of falling into a plain statement of the accidental nature of individual form.

GRANITE, on the other hand, is a very hard, granular substance, composed not, as marble, of a solid mass but rather of hard, coarse crystals. Because of its coarser structure, greater weight is implied than in a like piece of a softer stone. The working of granite differs considerably from marble and other solid stones, since it cannot be cut but must be pounded and crushed into shape. Hence a subject most suitable for this material would be one in which the maximum expression would be attained by a simplified, generalized statement, with no development of small, subtle planes, and no amount of detail to speak of, a subject for which the expression of mass and volume were important.

THEREFORE, the statement of form in its permanent character is most compatible with granite; and even though a high polish is obtainable, when used it should emphasize the broad, general planes and areas of the surfaces, rather than, as in marble, the play of light over small planes. A good example of a work in granite can be seen in the "Torso" by Zorach in the Whitney Museum (Plate 30). In this, the subject matter is most suitably adapted to an expression of the qualities of the material.

THE use of wood has also figured prominently in his sculpture. Although a very easy material to carve, it nevertheless exerts through its grain a certain control over the sculptor. The character of wood varies from the extremely hard, heavy lignum vitae to the comparatively soft maple, and consequently the form adaptable to it must vary also. A generalized statement, with simplified forms, such as the "Figure of a Girl" (Plate 18), is an excellent example of his carving in the harder wood; while "Kiddie Car" (Plate 20), carved in rosewood, shows the greater development of form possible in a slightly softer wood. In either case, a certain decorative quality is possible, a freer handling of projections and silhouettes, while an expansion of form can be suggested because of the ease with which wood can be worked.

BRONZE is another material frequently used for sculpture. In this medium, forms modelled in clay can be translated into a permanent substance, preserving all of the character of the original. Capable of a very high polish, this material is particularly suitable for the rendering of a figure modelled in detail and defined by small, subtle planes which flow easily one into another. Hence forms may be rendered which preserve in permanent material a subject matter of original, spontaneous character, first worked out in clay. Sometimes the actual thumb marks of the modelling are recorded in the bronze; they can be seen in many of the portrait busts by Jacob Epstein. A more simplified surface, however, thought out first in clay with the fluid, smooth, decorative character of the finished bronze in mind, produces a work perhaps more expressive of the true possibilities of this material. Zorach has done comparatively few works in this medium, being primarily a direct carver and not a modeller.

45

THESE are the materials of sculpture principally used by him; and the extent to which he has studied their properties and character, and the extent to which he has selected his forms in accordance with this knowledge, will be clearly revealed in our examination of the marble "Mother and Child" (Plates 23 and 24).

EVEN though monumental in scale, this work was cut directly in the stone, a pink Spanish marble. This material is of a beautiful, rich color, with a minimum of veinings, and of a grain of medium fineness. Thus it lends itself to shapes expressive of an expanding volume, of delicate surface modelling by means of carefully arranged planes which break up the play of light over the surface and more completely interpret the form. The subject most completely suited to such a treatment is a nude form capable of great expressiveness. Zorach considered this when he wished to interpret the emotional relationship between mother and child; thus after careful deliberation he selected this particular marble as being the one in which the most complete realization of his idea could be attained.

THIS adaptation of form to material has been an important characteristic of his work from his early wood carvings to the present time. Moreover, a close relationship between the sculptor and his material has been one of the traits of the more original twentieth century sculptors, and one which distinguishes them from most of their predecessors of the nineteenth century. In this, they are related to certain periods of the past—such as the Egyptian, the archaic Greek, the early Mediaeval, and the ancient Chinese. Thus an understanding of materials and the forms appropriate to them has had a great influence on the style of modern sculpture; this has been especially true of the direct carvers, and Zorach is an eminent figure in this group.

LOOKING at the "Mother and Child," one is aware instantly of the large, ample forms. Compared with the more photographic examples of academic sculpture, these large forms at first glance seem inappropriate and disturbing. This treatment of form we have found to be common to all of Zorach's sculpture. The reason for it is two-fold: first, by such amplification he has counteracted the optical illusion of slender, lifeless figures which might have resulted if the forms were rendered in exact size; secondly, by this method he has given accent to the basic character of each form, which in turn gives a greater sense of plastic reality. Perhaps more important, however, is that by this means he renders the truly architectural structure of the human figure.

THE use of these ample forms, on the other hand, would be most unsatisfactory if they were rendered in a detailed, realistic fashion; instead, the sculptor closely analyzes the principal component parts of his figures and expresses these parts in simplified terms, so as to give the inherent character of each of them. Thus it is valid sculpturally to increase the size of these component parts, for in this way the structural importance of each part and the relationships between them are made clearer. Through this method is achieved a sense of amplified, expanding forms, that is, forms in which an expression of inner volume is so brought out that it creates a vital feeling of inner stress against the surface, giving a semblance of living structure to the forms. Furthermore, the texture and color of the Spanish marble of the "Mother and Child" lend themselves to such an expression.

NOT only has Zorach amplified his forms for the sake of greater sculptural emphasis, but he has also resorted to distortion and exaggeration. This can be seen at once in the large hands of the mother, and in the large left leg of this figure. In the case of the hands, this method is used to accentuate an important emotional element in the work, and also in the case of design to bind the mother and child into closer physical unity; whereas the leg accents the vertical character of the rhythm which pervades the entire work and carries the eye instantly up to the head and face of the mother and child. This use of exaggeration and distortion is another feature found in practically all of his work.

THE arrangement of the figures in this group shows the careful attention given to the primary element of design, the forms being so placed as to attain a maximum of expressiveness and retain the basic structural quality of the material. The work is designed around a central axis: from the base of the stone to the head of the mother the eye is carried up in a spiral movement. Consequently, the sculpture is truly three-dimensional: definitely existing in space. It is in accordance with this three-dimensionality that Zorach has arranged his forms. Closely intertwined, so as to emphasize the spiritual through the physical relationships between the mother and child, the figures create an interesting pattern and a constantly changing silhouette, as one moves about the work, in which the solid forms are no less used than the open spaces between them. A slow, solemn rhythm moves continuously around the single forms and through the entire group, a rhythm completely compatible with the idea of the group.

ALTHOUGH the individual forms are rendered in broad, general terms, the surfaces are refined and further developed by an infinite number of delicate, subtle planes, which are so logical in their arrangement as to enrich the description of the forms rather than to diminish the expression of volume and mass. These fine surface planes add greatly to the richness of the work and are a further example of Zorach's understanding of his material, a marble of the texture and color of this pink Spanish variety lending itself beautifully to just such developed surface modulations. Thus the work illustrates the sculptor's interpretation of a subject in terms of his material, the material in turn being suitable for the design and for the forms selected, so that, in fact, the group seems naturally to grow out of the stone, or, in other words, the stone seems to come to life in the forms.

As an interpretation of a subject, the "Mother and Child" is characteristic of the artist. He is concerned not with specific figures, but with the physical, emotional, and spiritual associations between them. Thus the purpose of this group

49

is not to render forms and types related to an age or a country, but to express in simplified, formal terms the constant and ageless elements in such a relationship. In an expression of this sort, the imitative recording of the characteristics of a model, and the dramatic or tragic implications of the subject could have no place. Instead, Zorach has presented calm and generalized figures, as contained emotionally as is the design within the compact enclosing silhouette.

NEVERTHELESS, the profound and sincere expression of a fundamental emotion is gained by designing the figures in so close an inter-relationship, and by such simple expedients as the position of the large, expressive hands of the mother in an attitude of tender protectiveness, and of the child's arms placed on her breast in a significant gesture of affection. Moreover, these qualities are further brought out by the serene, meditative expression on the face of the mother and by the eager and quizzically youthful expression on the face of the child.

THUS the effectiveness of this group does not come through the realistic description of feature or form, but rather through the clear and broad statement of the underlying conception. There is here, therefore, a complete unity between the idea, the forms used to convey that idea, and the material in which they are rendered.

THIS attitude towards subject matter, this preference for simplified, expansive forms, and this approach to materials are not peculiarities common to the "Mother and Child," but are the most significant elements in the calm and vigorously sculptural style of Zorach. The range of his subject matter has not thus far in his career been particularly wide, primarily because he has had opportunity to do but little sculpture for a particular purpose and a specific site, most of his work having been done out of personal desire. Because of this, his subject matter has been confined for the most part to his wife and children, his cats, and portraits of his friends, all rendered not in their individualistic aspects but in terms of their formal and structural characteristics. The features of his style are apparent in everything he does. A feeling for the essential, for the simple basic structure pervades all of his work; while a detached attitude, a calm and repose, comparable to that of the early Greek and Egyptian sculptures, further adds to the clarity and the grandeur of his work.

His figures give above all else an expression of life in stone —life in its intrinsic, eternal aspects, not as a naturalistic or realistic representation, but as expanded and enriched, adding to our experience of the possibilities and inherent qualities of nature. Life in its simple, human aspects supplies the themes of his sculpture. Through his understanding of form he analyzes these themes to determine their significant characteristics. These are then modified, emphasized and arranged in a design of structural compactness, in which a noble rhythm defines and unifies the elements of the forms, bringing out the spatial inter-relationships between them. Each essential part has its own volume and weight, and is necessary for the complete expression of the solid structural mass of the figure as a whole. The sculpture of Zorach represents that perfect fusion of material with subject matter—stone become life, and life rendered in the permanent qualities of stone.

6 Excerpts from His Writings: His Ideas and His Methods

ZORACH upon occasion contributes critical essays on the art of sculpture. Often they are in the nature of philosophic interpretations, often they are concerned with practical matters; in either case, they are interesting and instructive. The following excerpts have been selected from a few of his writings because they make clear his own ideas on sculpture in general and refer to his own works in particular, and because they contain his own statement on the nature of sculpture. The ideas which are here developed at some length have been dealt with in less detail in the preceding chapters.

On the Art of Sculpture

"... A human being who is naturally a real artist touches a piece of material and under his touch it becomes a thing of life. Another, who is not an artist, but just a workman, may do a perfectly executed piece of work but that thing is still-born. The layman is apt to confuse the two. He is led astray by his awe of mere craftsmanship and forgets that without art content a thing is meaningless. . ."—From *Direct Sculpture.**

"... Art is the expression of mankind, a universal and cosmic expression of the soul of man, an expression of the realness of the

*For these references see the Bibliography on pp. 66-68.

universe and life. Art is the soul of man, ever striving, ever straining toward some fulfilment, some consciousness of itself and life. . ."—From *The New Tendencies in Art*.

". . . To arrive at the true realization of sculpture the artist must have a great deal of experience cutting direct. In that way he chips away the surface, but there is always the weight and volume inside to balance. The actual resistance of tough material is a wonderful guide. He cannot make changes easily, there is no putting back tomorrow what was cut away today. . . Slowly the vision grows as the work progresses. . ."—From *Direct Sculpture*.

". . . For the artist to do a life size figure in stone requires at the least a year. In clay, he can make six life size figures in a year. . . Where art is concerned the element of time should not enter. . . Real creation comes by slow stages of development. But everybody and everything is rushing around us and we are driven by the mere psychological idea of speed; this is very destructive. You can't rush the birth of a child nor can you hurry the creation of a work of art. . ."—From *Direct Sculpture*.

". . . There are a great many ways of doing sculpture and there is no one way that is the right way. No person or age has had the perfect way. Their way may have been perfect for them, but that does not mean it is the right method for us. The means and forms differ, but the underlying basis or qualities are ever the same. The eternal desire of man to recreate himself in a more perfect image, physically or spiritually, or mystically is there in all races at all times. . ."—From *Direct Sculpture*.

". . . Sculpture is a very definite job in itself. It is not only evolving a beautiful design and a form, but it is the development of that form. It is sensitizing that form, projecting into the form a highly sensitized and emotional quality: that is the quality that I feel is lacking in most modern sculpture today..."—From *Modern Sculpture*.

"... The modern movement has freed art from the idea of reproducing nature ... which has suddenly been found to have nothing to do with art... The essential contribution of modern art ... is the building up and development of purely abstract forms... By abstract form I mean purely geometric shapes and simplified equivalents of nature,—such as an apple reduced to a circle, a head to an oval,—and the building up of ... a piece of sculpture by a combination of these forms, dissected and interlaced, interwoven and developed. Through this re-creation, this building up and eliminating of everything not vitally necessary, is built up a structure whole, is developed a harmony of form... Infinite possibilities of expression and beauty lie in the development of this subtle interplay of form, the disappearing and approaching of shapes and planes, the projections of solids and the dissembling and reassembling of forms... Handled by an artist, sensitive to feeling, to design, to the relations of form and color, they reveal an inner and outer construction and a spirituality that may give the spectator in turn a deeper realization, a consciousness of a new beauty."—From *The New Tendencies in Art*.

"... There is nothing particularly new in this modern art. It is based upon the same cosmic principles of harmonious balance and relation of lines, forms, colors, volumes as is all true art..."—From *The New Tendencies in Art*.

"... What is form? Form is something that can perhaps be described as an architectural arrangement, a design in three dimen-

55

sions, flowing in and out and around a solid which is a living, breathing mass charged with emotion, and moving, not only in the sense of not being static, but moving spiritually, emotionally, and usually mentally... There is no reason to do sculpture unless one is charged with this great and moving force..."—From *Creative Sculpture*.

"... There is no such thing as following the model in any real art, ancient or modern; an artist may use a model, either a figure or nature, but never literally follows it... The artist translates, interprets, continually selecting, discarding, altering, creating..." —From *The New Tendencies in Art*.

On the Making of Sculpture *

"THE principle of the use of tools for cutting stone is very simple and is the same today as it was before history. Thousands of years ago man chose a rock and with an implement pounded this rock until he got a semblance of form, and then with stones and abrasives, and much muscle and patience ground the rock down to a smooth and polished surface. We do the same today. We have a greater variety and knowledge of tools... but primitive people developed various methods of drilling and polishing not so different from ours today."

"... It is not the complicated tool or the variety of tools that counts... The most beautiful and finest work can be done by the simplest method and with the simplest tools—in the case of stone cutting, chisels, properly tempered, and hammers... of various shapes and sizes, according to the work... Tools must be kept

* The excerpts given in this section are from Zorach's article, *Tools and Materials: Carved Sculpture*.

sharp... The same tools cannot be used on both marble and granite. A granite tool has a blunt point, a marble tool a sharp one, and the tempers are different..."

"...I have no set rule of procedure in carving. Sometimes I let the stone suggest its possibilities. Sometimes I work from drawings. Sometimes I make a small rough model in clay; this gives me a mass or design and allows me freedom to develop my final form. I always feel free to change and follow the development of the forms as they grow. A small sketch in clay will give a sense of dimension and depth, of direction and planes..."

"...The process of roughing out granite or marble is very similar except that the marble should be cut, more or less, while the granite has to be crushed... From the outside edges you gradually work in, developing a semblance of form or mass of the figure or composition. The idea is not to work too fast but to chip off small pieces and to resist all temptation to develop detail until the larger forms are completely developed... As the form develops, the sculptor's blows become more subtle and the chisels he uses are smaller... Delicate parts such as nose, eyes, ears... must be cut on a bevel, each form developed on the order of a pyramid supported by a mass in back... In working marble the final finish can be developed by... just pushing the tool back and forth over the surface with a slow pressure. This chiseled surface is slow work but is much superior to a surface developed by files, rasps and sandpaper... Polishing should be done with great patience and feeling—otherwise, the planes are lost and the forms merely rounded off and destroyed. If a high polish is desired, the stone is rubbed with fine carborundum stones, with lump pumice and, finally, hones. The final rubbing is done with thick Mexican felt and putty powder (tin oxide)... Small areas are worked over at a time and not the whole surface at once..."

"... I believe in continual observation and study of nature, not from the point of view of copying but from the point of view of form relation and form development. You have to work long and hard at a thing for the inner form to reveal itself. People always ask, 'What do you do if you cut away too much?' The answer is, you don't; cutting is a constant balancing of form against form..."

"... To me, direct sculpture is greater than modelled sculpture; its problems are greater and its possibilities of creative expression are deeper. More goes into it, not just in time and work, but in creative thought and feeling..."

". . . There can be worthless direct carving as well as meaningless modelling. So much depends upon what the artist has to contribute that any individual work stands on its own merits whether carved direct or modelled..."

". . . In direct carving the artist is the sole master of his materials from the very first conception in roughing it out, to the final details and perfecting. And after all, who but the creator can really know what to do with a piece of creative work?"

7 Catalogue Raisonné

1917—(1) Decorative relief panel: draped figure, arms over head, against background of White Mountain Falls.
butternut wood; 6" × 14"
Mrs. Samuel Wolman, Baltimore, Md. *Plate 1*

1918—(2) Walking Baby
original in terra cotta, now broken; ca. 8"
4 bronze copies: Mrs. Resor, New York City; Mr. and Mrs. Laurence Rockefeller, New York City; Mrs. Malcolm McBride, Cleveland, Ohio; and possession of the artist *Plate 2*

1918—(3) Mother and Child: two relief medallions; terra cotta; ca. 8"
Mrs. Zelma Schubart, New York City; Rebecca Hourwich, Robin Hood, Maine.

1918—(4) Modelled and carved bowl, with figures; terra cotta; ca. 6" diameter
Owner unknown.

1919—(5) Man with Two Wives
cedarwood; 24"
Mrs. Nathan J. Miller, New Rochelle, N. Y. *Plate 3*

1920—(6) Artist's Daughter
sprucewood; ca. 8"
possession of artist *Plate 4*

1920—(7) Kneeling Child
sprucewood; ca. 6"
lost

1921—(8) Young Boy
maplewood; 24"
possession of artist *Plate 5*

1921—(9) Young Girl
mahogany; 24"
Dr. Kempf, New York City *Plate 6*

1921—(10) Figure of Child
maplewood; ca. 7"
Mr. Arthur Egner, President, Newark Museum, Newark, N. J.; 2 bronze copies: Holger Cahill, Washington, D. C.; Doris Hillman, Los Angeles, Cal. *Plate 7*

1922—(11) Floating Figure
mahogany; 3'
possession of artist *Plate 8*

1922—(12) Male and Female: 2 wood carvings, originally as fork and spoon; maplewood; ca. 6"—8"
Mr. and Mrs. Lathrop Brown, Montauk, or New York City

1922—(13) Mother and Child
(finished 1923); mahogany; 3'
Mr. and Mrs. Lathrop Brown,
Montauk, or New York City
Plate 9

1922—(14) Boy and Girl Group
mahogany; ca. 3'
Ralph Jonas, New York City
Plate 10

1922—Last oil painting

1923—(15) Portrait head of Artist's Daughter; marble; over
life-size
Mrs. Ellen Dupont Wheelwright, Wilmington, Del.
Plate 11

1923—(16) Head of Woman
pink Tennessee marble; ca. life-size
Newark Museum, Newark,
N. J. *Plate 12*

1923—(17) Head of Boy
bronze; life-size
Mrs. Ira M. Yonkers, White
Plains, N. Y.

1923—(18) Figure of Girl
(finished winter 1924); lignum
vitae; ca. 3½'—4'
Frank Crowninshield, New
York City *Plate 13*

1923—(19) Pegasus (finished
winter 1924); walnut; 20"
Whitney Museum of American
Art, New York City; Plaster
copy: Mrs. Edward Voss,
Mochton, Md. *Plate 14*

1923—(20) Kiddie Car (finished
winter 1924); rosewood; 18"—
20"
Possession of artist *Plate 15*

1924—(21) Figures and animals:
2 relief door-panels; walnut;
2' × 5' each—life-size
for Schwarzenbach Home, 9 E.
62nd St., New York City (now
The Whist Club House)
Plate 16

1924—(22) Head of Boy
applewood; over life-size
possession of artist *Plate 17*

1924—(23) Portrait head: Kenneth Nosker; bronze; life-size
Kenneth Nosker, New York
City

1924—(24) Cat (finished summer 1925); pink Tennessee
marble; over life-size
Schwarzenbach Collection

1924—(25) Portrait Head of
Mrs. Zorach (finished summer
1926); pink Tennessee marble;
slightly over life-size
possession of artist *Plate 18*

1924—(26) Head of Boy
granite; over life-size
possession of artist

1925—(27) Head of Girl
lignum vitae; over life-size
possession of artist

1925—(28) Draped Female Figure; teakwood; ca. 10″
Mrs. William L'Engle, New York City; bronze copies: Dr. H. M. Friedman, New York City; Mr. Paul Lamb, Shaker Heights, Ohio

1925—(29) Clock, with three figures (finished 1926); bronze; 5′ square
for top of Schwarzenbach Building (now Stewart Building), 32nd Street and Fourth Avenue, New York City

1926—(30) Reclining Cat
mahogany; over life-size
Mrs. John Steube; bronze copy: possession of artist

1926—(31) Head of Woman (finished 1927); granite; slightly over life-size
possession of artist

1926—(32) Cat
mahogany; life-size
Dr. and Mrs. Nathan Krass, wood and gesso copy: Edsel Ford; plaster copy: possession of artist; bronze copy: Mrs. Jane Rogers, New York City

1926—(33) Decorative doors
bronze; 2 panels, each 7′ × 2½′
Schwarzenbach Building (now Stewart Building), 32nd Street and Fourth Avenue, New York City

1926—(34) Child with Cat
pink Tennessee marble; over life-size
possession of artist; bronze copies: Leonore Kroll, New York City; Mrs. B. Goldsmith, South Salem, Conn. *Plate 19*

1927—(35) Portrait of Robert Schwarzenbach; yellow marble; over life-size
possession of artist

1927—(36) Head of Girl
bronze; ca. 5″
possession of artist

1927—(37) Family Group: 2 relief panels; Brazilian walnut; 2′ × 5″
possession of artist *Plate 20*

1927—(38) Figure of Child
white Italian marble; 18″
D. Sakatwalla, Pittsburgh, Penna.; bronze copies: Evelyn Ferdeber, New York City; Edith Halpert, New York City

1927—(39) Figure of Young Girl in Short Dress
maplewood; 4′
Berkshire Museum, Pittsfield, Mass. *Plate 21*

1927—(40) Figure of Young Girl in Short Dress
teakwood; 12″
possession of artist

1927—(41) Mother and Child
bronze sketch; ca. 18″
possession of artist; copy: David
L. Loewe, Hollywood, California   *Plate 22*

1927—(42) Mother and Child
(began spring 1927, finished
winter 1930); Spanish Rosa
marble; 5½′ high (1½ life-size)
possession of artist *Plates 23, 24*

1928—(43) Girl in Short Dress
with Cat
teakwood; ca. 12″
Ralph Jonas, New York City

(During 1928 worked mostly on
large "Mother and Child")

1929—(44) Kneeling Girl
bronze; 3′
Mrs. Wheelwright, Wilmington, Del.

1929—(45) Torso
brownstone; 15″
Mrs. John Steube, Columbus,
Ohio

1929—(46) Standing Girl, with
arms over head; bronze; 10″
possession of artist; copy;
George Hourwich, New York
City

1929—(47) "Allegory," over-
mantel relief panel; Brazilian
walnut; ca. 4′ × 5′
Ralph Jonas, New York City

1929—(48) "History of California"—relief panel; plaster
sketch model for frieze for Los
Angeles City Hall
possession of artist   *Plate 25*

(During 1929 worked intensely
on large "Mother and Child")

1930—(49) Artist's Daughter—
three-quarter figure, arms folded
Georgia pink marble; life-size
Whitney Museum of American
Art, New York City   *Plate 26*

1930—(50) Bunny
granite boulder; life-size
Whitney Museum of American
Art, New York City

1930—(51) Mother and Child
bronze; ca. 10″
Dr. Wade, New York City

1930—(52) "The Dance," decorative panel: bronze; 6″ × 8″
possession of artist, bronze
copies: Mrs. Louis Stern, New
York City; Mrs. Irwin Shapiro,
New York City

1930—(53) Portrait of Phillip
Wittenberg; bronze; life-size
Phillip Wittenberg, Brooklyn,
N. Y.

1930—(54) Portrait of Dr. H.
M. Friedman; plaster; life-size
possession of artist

1930—(55) Guinea-pigs
pink Tennessee marble; over
life-size
possession of artist

(The large "Mother and Child"
finished winter 1930)

1931—(56) Portrait: "Hilda"
Jaune Nile marble; over life-size
Mrs. Etta Cone, Baltimore, Md.
Plate 27

1931—(57) Portrait of Edith
Halpert
Jaune Nile marble; over life-size
possession of artist

1931—(58) Football Player
granite; life-size
On loan to Newark Museum,
Newark, N. J.; plaster copy:
possession of artist

1931—(59) Cat
natural green boulder; life-size
Mrs. J. D. Rockefeller, Jr.,
New York City   *Plate 28*

1932—(60) Portrait of Weyhe
son; plaster; life-size
Weyhe, New York City

1932—(61) Spirit of the Dance
cast aluminum; twice life-size
Music Hall, Rockefeller Center,
New York City; bronze copy:
on loan to Brooklyn Museum,
Brooklyn, N. Y.; plaster orig-
inal: possession of artist
Plate 29

1932—(62) Torso
Labrador granite; life-size
Whitney Museum of American
Art, New York City   *Plate 30*

1932—(63) Small Torso
white marble; ca. 15"
possession of artist

1932—(64) "Flora and Fauna of
Maine"—12 relief panels; teak-
wood; 20" × 24"—10" × 36"
Panelling for library of Mrs.
O'Brien, Detroit, Michigan

1932—(65) Child Drinking
bronze; ca. 8"
possession of artist   *Plate 31*

1933—(66) Affection
York Fossil; ca. 3'
possession of artist   *Plate 32*

1933—(67) The Embrace
plaster; 1½ life-size
possession of artist   *Plate 33*

1933—(68) Rabbit
granite boulder; life-size
Miss Helen Frick, New York
City

1933—(69) Head
granite; life-size
possession of artist   *Plate 34*

1933—(70) Seated Girl
bluestone; ca. 5" × 6"
possession of artist   *Plate 35*

1933—(71) Decorative circular relief panel, with two figures bronze; 15″ × 10″
possession of artist; Mr. Nelson Rockefeller, New York City

1934—(72) Portrait of Katharine Shanahan; marble; over life-size
Dr. Shanahan, Brooklyn, N. Y.
Plate 36

1934—(73) Lenin Memorial plaster sketch model; 3′
submitted to Commission at Moscow, but never returned to artist *Plates 37, 37a*

1934—(74) Bathing Girl Borneo mahogany; 4′
possession of artist *Plate 38*

1934—(75) Frog granite boulder; over life-size
Mr. Nelson Rockefeller, New York City

1934—(76) Hound granite boulder; life-size
possession of artist *Plate 39*

1934—(77) Child on Pony York Fossil; ca. 20″
possession of artist *Plate 40*

1935—(78) Youth mahogany; life-size
possession of artist *Plate 41*

1935—(79) "Conflict" — two pendant figures; plaster; 1½ life-size
possession of artist

1935—(80) Portrait of Mrs. Hillman; bronze; life-size
Mrs. Hillman, New York City

1935—(81) Portrait of Elsa Voss plaster; life-size
possession of artist

1935—(82) Pigeon granite boulder; life-size
Mr. Laurence Rockefeller, New York City; bronze copy: Iskander Hourwich, New York City

1935—(83) Setting Hen white marble; twice life-size
possession of artist

1935—(84) Cat granite; 1½ life-size
possession of artist *Plate 42*

1935—(85) Sleeping Dog granite boulder; life-size
possession of artist

1935—(86) "Friendship": decorative panel; bronze; ca. 6″ × 12″
possession of artist

1936—(87) The Speer Memorial plaster sketch; 40″
submitted in competition for the Speer Memorial, Denver, Colorado *Plate 43*

1936—(88) Portrait of Dr. Shanahan; bronze; slightly over life-size
Dr. Shanahan, Brooklyn, N. Y.

1936—(89) Portrait head of Dahlov Zorach; granite boulder; over life-size
possession of artist

1936—(90) Portrait of Basil Shanahan; bronze; slightly over life-size
Dr. Shanahan, Brooklyn, N. Y.

1936—(91) Standing figure of Abraham Lincoln
Plaster sketch; ca. 20"
possession of artist

1936—(92) Cat (finished 1937) granite; ca. 18"
Metropolitan Museum of Art, New York City   Plate 44

1936—(93) Full-length figure of Abraham Lincoln; plaster sketch model; 18" — 20"
possession of artist   Plate 45

1937—(94) Pioneer Family Group (in nude)
plaster model; 30"
submitted in Dallas, Texas, competition; now in possession of artist   Plate 46

1937—(95) Pioneer Family Group (clothed)
plaster model; 30"
submitted in Dallas, Texas, competition; now in possession of artist

1937—(96) Benjamin Franklin: full-length standing figure (started in 1935); Tennessee marble; 7½'
Reception Hall, Benjamin Franklin Post Office, Washington, D. C.   Plate 47

1937—(97) Fountain of Horses plaster sketch model; figures ca. 8", entire fountain ca. 20" × 80"
possession of artist   Plate 48

1937—(98) Male and Female reclining group
Juane Nile marble; two thirds life-size
(started during summer of 1934; will finish during summer of 1938)   Plate 49

8 Bibliography

A SELECTIVE bibliography of some of the more important critical writings (a) on Zorach and (b) by Zorach. For further references the reader should consult The Index of Twentieth Century Artists, the Art Index and the indices of The Art News and The Art Digest.

(a) Writings on Zorach

GENERAL SOURCES

Cahill, Holger & Barr, Alfred H., Jr., editors—Art in America in Modern Times, New York, 1934, pp. 37, 56-57; 2nd ed. enlarged, Art in America: A Complete Survey, New York, 1935, pp. 95, 114-115.

Hudnut, Joseph—Contemporary Sculpture, Fairmount Park Art Association, Philadelphia, 1933.

LaFollette, Suzanne—Art in America, New York & London, 1929, pp. 333, 343.

Moore, Dorothy Lefferts—William Zorach (Art Portfolio Series), New York, 1931, 12 plates.

Neuhaus, Eugen—The History and Ideals of American Art, Stanford University Press, California, and Oxford University Press, London, 1931, p. 360.

Parkes, Kineton—The Art of Carved Sculpture, New York & London, 1931, Vol. I, pp. 150-153.

Phillips, Duncan—A Collection in the Making, New York, 1926, p. 71.

BIBLIOGRAPHY

ARTICLES

Barr, Alfred H., Jr., editor—Modern Works of Art. Museum of Modern Art Exhibition Catalogue, New York, 1934, pp. 18, 19.

Brenner, Anita—Zorach and Modern Art, *Menorah Journal*, Vol. 16, New York, 1929, pp. 322-324.

Cahill, Holger—William Zorach. Catalogue of Exhibition: "Recent Sculpture by William Zorach," The Downtown Gallery, New York, January 27-February 15, 1931.

Cahill, Holger—American Painting and Sculpture. Museum of Modern Art Exhibition Catalogue, New York, October 31, 1932-January 31, 1933, p. 21.

Cross, Louise—William Zorach, *London Studio*, Vol. 8, London, 1934, pp. 80-82.

Flint, Ralph—Zorach's Work at the Downtown Gallery, *The Art News*, Vol. 29, New York, January 31, 1931, p. 6.

Kellow, F. L.—Zorach's Sculpture, *The Survey*, Vol. 66, New York, April 1, 1931, p. 40.

Knowlton, Walter—Around the Galleries, *Creative Art*, Vol. 8, New York, March 1931, sup. 84-85.

Mannes, Marya—Exhibition, Downtown Gallery, *The International Studio*, Vol. 98, New York, March 1931, p. 74.

Strawn, Arthur—The Zorachs, *The Outlook*, Vol. 157, New York, February 11, 1931, p. 236.

Villar, Mariquita—William Zorach and His Sculpture, *Parnassus*, Vol. 6, New York, October 1934, pp. 3-6.

(b) Writings by Zorach

The New Tendencies in Art, *The Arts*, Vol. 2, New York, October 1921, pp. 10-15.

The Sculpture of Edgar Degas, *The Arts,* Vol. 8, New York, November 1925, pp. 263-265.

The Sculpture of Constantin Brancusi, *The Arts,* Vol. 9, March 1926, pp. 143-150.

The Artist's Point of View, *Bulletin, New York City Art Center,* Vol. 8, June 1930, pp. 126-127.

Direct Sculpture, A paper read at the Town Hall Club, New York City, February 1930.

The Child and Art, *The Arts,* Vol. 16, February, 1930, pp. 394-397.

Views and Methods, *Creative Art,* Vol. 6, New York, June 1930, pp. 443-445.

Modern Sculpture, A paper read at the Art Students League, New York City, December 1931.

Nationalism in Art—Is it an Advantage? (Whitney Museum Debate), *The Art Digest,* Vol. 6, New York, March 15, 1932, pp. 15, 21-22.

Sculpture, *National Encyclopedia,* editor Henry Suzzallo, Vol. 9, New York, 1933, pp. 115-121.

Creative Sculpture, A paper read at the Finch School, New York City, April 1935.

Tools and Materials, IIc: Carved Sculpture, *American Magazine of Art,* Vol. 28, Washington, D. C., March 1935, pp. 156-160.

9 The Principal Exhibitions of Zorach's Sculpture

1924   —Kraushaar Gallery, New York City.

1926   —Kraushaar Gallery, New York City.

1928   —Kraushaar Gallery, New York City.

1930–31—Museum of Modern Art, New York City.

1931   —Downtown Gallery, New York City.

1932–33—Museum of Modern Art, New York City.

1933   —Chicago Art Institute, Chicago, Ill.

1933   —Pennsylvania Museum of Art, Philadelphia, Penna.

1933   —Whitney Museum of American Art, New York City.

1934   —Chicago Art Institute (A Century of Progress), Chicago, Ill.

1934   —Museum of Modern Art, New York City.

1935   —Chicago Art Institute (A Century of Progress), Chicago, Ill.

1936   —Memorial Art Gallery, Rochester, N. Y.

1936   —Whitney Museum of American Art, New York City.

1936   —Wilmington Public Library Gallery, Wilmington, Del.

1937   —Passedoit Gallery, New York City.

1937   —Museum of Fine Arts, Cleveland, Ohio.

1937 —Milch Gallery, New York City.
1938 —Pennsylvania Academy of Fine Arts, Philadelphia, Penna.
1938 —Whitney Museum of American Art, New York City.

10 List of Photographs

* The numbers in parentheses refer to the Catalogue Raisonné, on pp. 59-65, where complete facts concerning these works are given.

Plate 19—(34) 1926: Child with Cat

Plate 20—(37) 1927: Family Group: two relief panels

Plate 21—(39) 1927: Figure of Young Girl in Short Dress

Plate 22—(41) 1927: Mother and Child

Plate 23—(42) 1927–30: Mother and Child—front view

Plate 24—(42) 1927–30: Mother and Child—back view

Plate 25—(48) 1929: History of California—relief panel (drawing)

Plate 26—(49) 1930: Artist's Daughter—three-quarter figure, arms folded

Plate 27—(56) 1931: Portrait—Hilda

Plate 28—(59) 1931: Cat

Plate 29—(61) 1932: Spirit of the Dance (plaster)

Plate 30—(62) 1932: Torso in Labrador Granite

Plate 31—(65) 1932: Child Drinking

Plate 32—(66) 1933: Affection

Plate 33—(67) 1933: The Embrace

Plate 34—(69) 1933: Granite Head

Plate 35—(70) 1933: Seated Girl

Plate 36—(72) 1934: Portrait of Katharine Shanahan

Plate 37—(73) 1934: Lenin Memorial

Plate 37a–(73) 1934: Detail—Lenin Memorial

Plate 38—(74) 1934: Bathing Girl

Plate 39—(76) 1934: Granite Hound

LIST OF PHOTOGRAPHS

Index

An index to the sculptures of Zorach discussed in the text.

Plate I (1)—1917—DECORATIVE RELIEF PANEL:
Draped figure, arms over head, against background
of White Mountain Falls.

*This was begun as a wood-block but soon developed into a relief
carving. It was cut from Butternut wood which had been part of
an old bureau drawer, and was made on an abandoned farm, the
Echo Farm, in New Hampshire.*

Plate 2 (2)—1918—WALKING BABY

A bronze copy of a terra cotta figure made during the summer of 1918 in New Hampshire, when Zorach had access to a kiln. The idea to do a figure came after much experimentation with firing pottery.

Plate 3 (5)—1919—MAN WITH TWO WIVES

This group was cut from a three-pronged cedar post which was to have been used as a supporting post for a house.

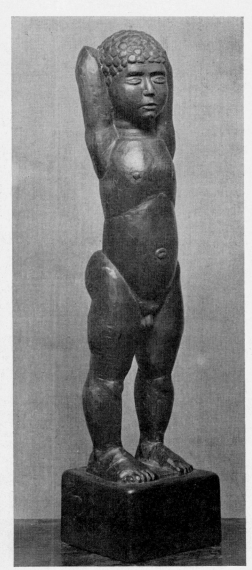

Plate 4 (6)—1920—
ARTIST'S DAUGHTER

While camping in Yosemite National Park, Zorach carved this little figure with a penknife, from sprucewood cut there.

Plate 5 (8)—1921—
YOUNG BOY

A figure based on the artist's small son; and carved in Provincetown from maplewood which the sculptor had brought back from California.

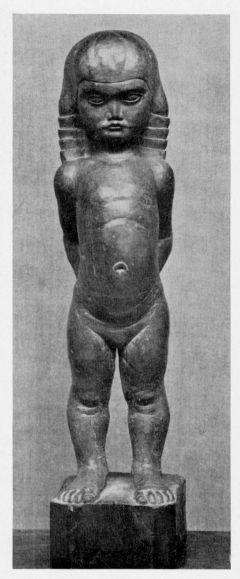

Plate 6 (9)—1921—
YOUNG GIRL

This work was also done in Provincetown, with the sculptor's young daughter serving as model. It is cut in African mahogany, which Zorach had bought from an old ship's carpenter, who had brought it from Africa about forty years earlier.

Plate 7 (10)—1921—
FIGURE OF A CHILD

Carved mostly with a penknife, as many of his earliest works were, this is practically a portrait of the sculptor's young daughter.

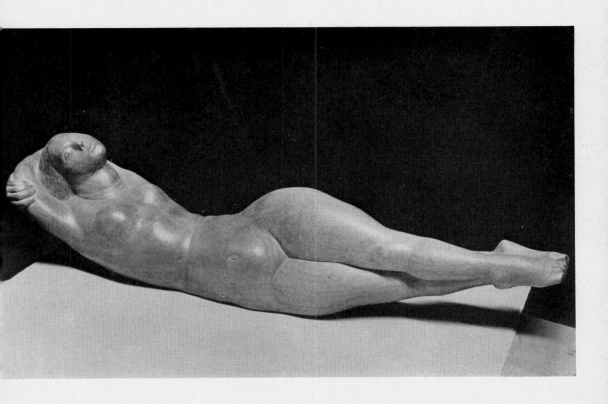

Plate 8 (11)—1922—FLOATING FIGURE

Carved from a piece of the African mahogany acquired from the ship's carpenter (see note under Plate 6), the shape of the block contributed to the development of the design. While this work was in the process of creation, Zorach was doing much swimming, and the observations made of forms in the water are reflected in this work.

Plate 9 (13)—1922—MOTHER AND CHILD

The Mother and Child motive had interested Zorach for some time:
he had made some comparatively unsuccessful attempts to present
the idea in painting, and this mahogany group is the first of his
efforts to develop the theme in sculpture.

Plate 10 (16)—1922—BOY AND GIRL GROUP

This group, carved in mahogany, grew from studies made of the sculptor's children.

Plate 11 (14)—1923—HEAD—ARTIST'S DAUGHTER

Carved in Provincetown from white Italian marble purchased in Boston, this was Zorach's first work in stone. It was cut directly in the marble and developed from many drawings made by the artist of his daughter.

Plate 12 (15)—1923—HEAD OF A WOMAN

This work was based on drawings made as studies of two persons. It was cut in pink Tennessee marble at Provincetown during the summer of 1923.

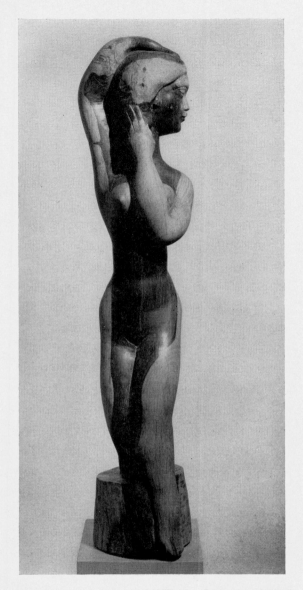

Plate 13 (18)—1923—FIGURE OF A GIRL

*The wood for this figure (lignum vitae) was purchased from a man
who had picked it up in the street, mistaking it for boxwood and
intending to make of it handles for tools. Zorach, at that time
interested in experimenting with woods, produced from it one of
the earliest of modern lignum vitae figures. This wood, very hard
and heavy, and sometimes called "iron-wood," has a black core and
the sculptor used this in working out his form.*

Plate 14 (19)—1923—PEGASUS

This group was carved from a square block of walnut, the sculptor adapting his design to the original shape of the block, preserving the solid compactness of it in his finished work.

Plate 15 (20)—1923—KIDDIE CAR

Carved in rosewood, this figure, like so many of Zorach's works of this period, is based on studies made of his young children.

Plate 16 (21)—1924—FIGURES AND ANIMALS:
Two Relief Door Panels

These panels are cut in two-inch thick Brazilian walnut. The designs show an interesting combination of convex and concave surfaces, preserving at the same time the original surface of the wood.

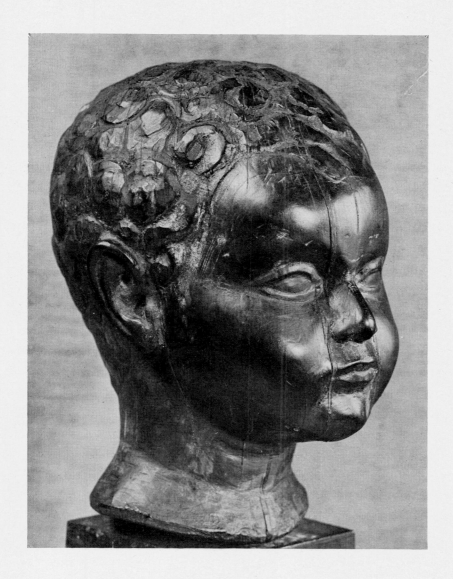

Plate 17 (22)—1924—HEAD OF A BOY

This small head has the richness and color of fine mahogany, although it is actually carved in light-colored but very hard apple-wood. While working on this head, the wood began to "check" or crack and when it was completed, and as an experiment, Zorach boiled it in linseed oil, which gave it this rich mahogany quality.

Plate 18 (25)—1924—PORTRAIT OF MRS. ZORACH

A direct carving in pink Tennessee marble, the color of the stone —a diffused grey-pink—gives a greater warmth and life-like quality to this head than would a white marble.

Plate 19 (34)—1926—CHILD WITH CAT

*Another example of Zorach's direct carving in stone. No prelimi-
nary sketches of any sort were made for this work, and the design
changed and developed as the sculptor progressed with his carving
and began to realize the possibilities of the shape and quality of the
stone.*

Plate 20 (37)—1927—FAMILY GROUP:
Two Relief Panels

*A decorative design in flat, low relief, cut in two-inch thick
Brazilian walnut.*

Plate 21 (39)—1927—FIGURE OF YOUNG GIRL
IN SHORT DRESS

*Based on studies made of his daughter, this figure was carved in
light-colored, hard maplewood, which was taken from a tree that
had blown down in a storm in Bath, Maine, during the summer
of 1927.*

Plate 22 (41)—1927—MOTHER AND CHILD

*Made as a clay sketch, and later cast in bronze, this work was a
preliminary study in the development of the "Mother and Child"
motive towards a larger work, which was begun the same year.*

Plate 23 (42)—1927-30—MOTHER AND CHILD—
Front View

The first monumental piece of sculpture done by Zorach, and his best known work. The culmination of years of study of the "Mother and Child" motive, this large group was freely cut directly in the marble, with no pointing or copying of a full-sized plaster model; but developed from a small sketch and grew by slow stages over a period of three years. As is generally true of his sculpture, is is entirely by his hand.

Plate 24 (42)—1927-30—MOTHER AND CHILD—
Back View

(see note under Plate 23)

Plate 25 (48)—1929—HISTORY OF CALIFORNIA:
Drawing for a Relief Panel

A drawing for a frieze which was to have been 90 feet long and 9 feet high, for the Los Angeles City Hall. It represents in symbolical fashion the history of California from primitive to modern times, using postures to express ideas, rather than mere description. This was never carried out, due to the stress of the then approaching economic depression.

Plate 26 (49)—1930—ARTIST'S DAUGHTER:
Three-quarter figure, arms folded

*Carved directly in Georgia pink marble, a brittle stone, this work
grew from a small sketch.*

Plate 27 (56)—1931—PORTRAIT: "HILDA"

*A direct carving made from drawings and from life-studies with
no preliminary sketches. The stone, a pale, yellowish Italian marble,
of great warmth and rich texture, is seldom used now for figure
carving, being mostly used for tombstones. It was from this type
of marble that an ancient Egyptian carved the magnificent Queen
Hatshepsut now in the Metropolitan Museum of Art in New York
City.*

Plate 28 (59)—1931—CAT

Always interested in the inherent quality and texture of stones, Zorach has done considerable experimentation with natural stones picked up at random in Maine. This represents such a work: ground by hand from a very hard natural green granite boulder, made directly without any preliminary sketch, but with the form developing as the work progressed.

Plate 29 (61)—1932—SPIRIT OF THE DANCE

Originally modelled in clay (from which this photograph was made) and later cast in aluminum, this work was done under commission for the Radio City Music Hall in New York City. When it was first exhibited, however, considerable controversy developed over the nudity of the figure, and for some months it disappeared from view. But during this time, the original clay model was exhibited at several places and received such favorable comments from the critics and the general public that the aluminum figure re-appeared in the Music Hall, where it is now a fixture, although badly placed.

Plate 30 (62)—1932—TORSO IN LABRADOR
GRANITE

*A work based on a fairly complete and worked out model, and
made from a very hard, grey Labrador granite.*

Plate 31 (65)—1932—CHILD DRINKING

Made considerably later from an earlier drawing of one of the sculptor's children.

Plate 32 (66)—1933—AFFECTION

Cut directly in York fossil, a dark blue-black marble, the sculptor working without a model and relying on a quick memory sketch of an actual happening.

Plate 33 (67)—1933—THE EMBRACE

This is a monumental clay sketch, which is both modelled and carved. It is the sculptor's desire to render this work later in stone.

Plate 34 (69)—1933—GRANITE HEAD

A direct carving based on preliminary pencil studies.

Plate 35 (70)—1933—SEATED GIRL

*This very small figure was made from a bluestone picked up by the
sculptor while walking along a road in Maine. The stone is very
hard and of the sandstone species, but has the character of granite.*

Plate 36 (72)—1934—PORTRAIT OF
KATHARINE SHANAHAN

Of white Greek Pentelic marble, this portrait was carved directly in the stone without any preliminary clay studies: occasionally the sculptor worked with the subject before him, and at other times he made pencil drawings as studies for the work in stone.

Plate 37 (73)—1934—LENIN MEMORIAL

A three-foot plaster sketch model which Zorach submitted to the Moscow commission in charge of the competition for a memorial to Lenin in Leningrad. It was the first monumental competition in which the sculptor took part. The entire monument was to have been 360 feet high, with the first base 75 feet and the second one about 60 feet. This project was never carried out by the Soviet Government, nor was the model ever returned to Zorach.

Plate 37a *(73)*—1934—DETAIL: LENIN MEMORIAL

(see note under Plate 37)

Plate 38 (74)—1934—BATHING GIRL

Cut from a piece of Borneo mahogany purchased by the sculptor from a German who had cut the tree in Borneo. When he bought the wood (a very heavy, hard species) it was already chopped into a rough shape, and into this the sculptor worked his figure.

Plate 39 (76)—1934—GRANITE HOUND

Made from a natural granite boulder picked up in a field in Maine. Zorach's preference for natural granite over quarried granite is because of its greater variety of color and texture.

Plate 40 (77)—1934—CHILD ON PONY

A direct carving in York fossil. For this the sculptor used no model but worked from drawings and pencil studies.

Plate 41 *(78)*—1935—YOUTH

*Also cut from Borneo mahogany acquired from the same source
as the wood used for the "Bathing Girl" (see Plate 38).*

Plate 42 (84)—1935—GRANITE CAT

*Made from a natural Maine boulder which the sculptor dug up in a
gravel pit. He has retained here as much as possible the natural
shape of the stone.*

Plate 43 (87)—1936—THE SPEER MEMORIAL

In collaboration with a Denver architect, Zorach submitted these plaster sketch models in the competition for this Memorial. In the final award he received first mention. The work has not been carried out.

Plate 44 (92)—1936—GRANITE CAT

This cat is made of quarried Swedish granite, and resulted from many studies and a great many drawings which the sculptor had made of a cat ("Tooky") that had been in the family for nine years.

Plate 45 (93)—1936—ABRAHAM LINCOLN

A plaster sketch model of the artist's conception of Lincoln, based on close studies of the character and personality of the man.

Plate 46 (94)—1937—PIONEER FAMILY GROUP

This plaster model was submitted in the Dallas competition of 1937, and, as was the case in the Denver competition of the year before, Zorach was awarded first mention by the judges; but public opinion rejected the group, primarily because of its nudity (even though a clothed group had been submitted by that time), and the final award was given to another sculptor.

Plate 47 (96)—1937—BENJAMIN FRANKLIN

Made from many small sketches and a full-sized plaster model, this figure in Tennessee marble is now in the Benjamin Franklin Post Office in Washington, D. C. In an effort to know the character and personality of the man, Zorach made many researches, which included old drawings and engravings, past statues of Franklin, the reading of his autobiography, and even an examination of the clothes he wore.

Plate 48 (97)—1937—FOUNTAIN OF HORSES

A preliminary sketch model for a fountain designed for a projected collaborative community center project—in which architects, sculptors, and painters were to have collaborated.

Plate 49 (98)—1938—MALE AND FEMALE: RECLINING GROUP

This is the work Zorach is at present bringing to completion. It is a direct carving in a beautiful Italian marble, and has developed from the small clay sketch, of which this is a photograph.